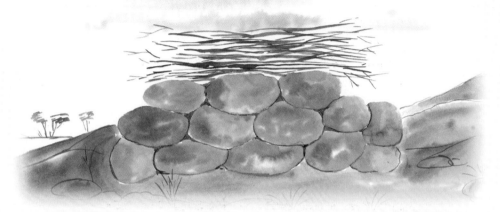

# THE BRAVE BOY

## Quran Stories for Little Hearts

by

SANIYASNAIN KHAN

Goodwordkidz

*Helping you build a family of faith*

Long long ago, about 4000 years ago, there lived the Prophet Ibrahim ﷺ (Abraham). He was gracious, tender-hearted and pure in faith. His family lived in a beautiful valley, which is now known as Makkah.

One night, the Prophet Ibrahim ﻋﻠﻴﻪ ﺍﻟﺴﻼﻡ dreamt that he was sacrificing his son, Ismail ﻋﻠﻴﻪ ﺍﻟﺴﻼﻡ. This was an order from his Lord.

5

Ismail ﷺ was still a child, but the Prophet Ibrahim ﷺ told him about the dream.

Ismail ﷿ was a brave boy. He was ready to obey the command of Allah, who had created him.

8

So without hesitating, he said to his father, "Do what you are commanded, father. God willing, you will find me one of the steadfast."

Ibrahim ﷺ took his son away to sacrifice him. As he reached a place, which is now known as Mina—a valley near Makkah—Satan appeared and tried to stop him from doing his Lord's bidding.

The Prophet Ibrahim ﷺ picked up
a few small stones and threw
them at Satan. Little Ismail ﷺ
and his mother did likewise.

The Prophet Ibrahim  gently placed his son on the ground and blindfolded himself with a handkerchief so that he could not see his beloved son while carrying out the Lord's command.

As Ibrahim عليه السلام took a knife to sacrifice Ismail عليه السلام, Allah sent the angel Jibril (Gabriel) down with a ram. "Sacrifice this ram. Do not sacrifice Ismail," said Jibril to Ibrahim عليه السلام.

Allah was so pleased with the readiness of Ibrahim عليه السلام to sacrifice his beloved son, that He commanded the believers to observe this day as Id al-Adha or the Feast of sacrifice. Every year Muslims sacrifice an animal in remembrance of the Prophet Ibrahim's trust in Allah.

This story reminds believers
of the readiness of the
Prophet Ibrahim ﷺ to give
up his most beloved son.

Likewise, believers should be ready to part with their precious belongings, and their wealth, and even give up their lives, if the cause of Islam so requires.

Thus the Quran says: "Truly, my prayers, my sacrifice, my life and my death all belong to Allah, the Lord of the Worlds". (*Surah al-Anam*, 6:162)

**Find Out More**
To know more about the message and meaning of Allah's words, look up the following parts of the Quran which tell the story of the Prophet Ibrahim ﷺ:

*Surah as-Saffat 37:102-111*

ﷺ *Alayhis Salam* 'May peace be upon him.' The customary blessings on the prophets.